this OR that?

weather

hail

OR

freezing rain?

Josh Plattner

Consulting Editor, Diane Craig, M.A./Reading Specialist

Super Sandcastle

An Imprint of Abdo Publishing
abdopublishing.com

abdopublishing.com

Printed in the United States of America, North Mankato, Minnesota

102015

012016

THIS BOOK CONTAINS
RECYCLED MATERIALS

Editor: Liz Salzmann

Content Developer: Nancy Tuminelly

Cover and Interior Design and Production: Mighty Media, Inc.

Photo Credits: Kelly Doudna, NOAA, Shutterstock

Library of Congress Cataloging-in-Publication Data

Plattner, Josh, author.

 Hail or freezing rain? / Josh Plattner ; consulting editor, Diane Craig.

   pages cm -- (This or that? Weather)

 ISBN 978-1-62403-954-6

1. Hail--Juvenile literature. 2. Freezing rain--Juvenile literature. I. Craig, Diane, editor. II. Title.

 QC929.H15.P53 2016

 551.57'87--dc23

                        2015020596

Super SandCastle™ books are created by a team of professional educators, reading specialists, and content developers around five essential components—phonemic awareness, phonics, vocabulary, text comprehension, and fluency—to assist young readers as they develop reading skills and strategies and increase their general knowledge. All books are written, reviewed, and leveled for guided reading and early reading intervention programs for use in shared, guided, and independent reading and writing activities to support a balanced approach to literacy instruction.

contents

hail or freezing rain?

Is it hail? Or is it freezing rain?
Do you know the difference?

Hail falls from the sky. It is ice.
It freezes before it lands.

Freezing rain falls from the sky. It is water. It freezes after it lands.

frosty forms

Each piece of hail is called a hailstone. Some hailstones are small. Some are large.

Freezing rain falls as water.
Then it freezes on things.
It forms a layer of ice.

7

how did it start?

Hail happens in the summer. It forms inside large thunderstorms.

Freezing rain happens in cold weather. It comes from winter storms.

created in clouds

Hail forms in a storm cloud. Each hailstone starts as a tiny piece of ice. Air swirls the ice around in the cloud. Water **droplets** freeze to it.

size grows

tiny piece of ice

heavy enough to fall

hail

The hailstone gets bigger and bigger. It gets heavier. Finally, it falls to the ground.

Freezing rain begins as snow or rain. It falls toward the ground. First it goes through warmer air. The snow melts. It turns into rain.

Then the rain falls through cold air.
It becomes very cold. The cold rain
freezes when it hits something.

cold and coated

A hailstone can be as small as a pea. It can be as big as a softball. The largest hailstone was 8 inches (20.3 cm). It weighed almost 2 pounds (.9 kg)! It fell in South Dakota.

Freezing rain makes a layer of ice. The layer of ice is called glaze. It is clear. It is smooth.

double danger

Hail dents cars. A large hailstone can **crack** glass. It can hurt people.

Glaze from freezing rain is **slippery**. It makes it hard to drive or walk.

what happened here?

A hailstorm can ruin crops.
Hailstones knock down the plants.

A thick layer of ice is heavy. Tree branches and power lines can break.

at a glance

hail —————— freezing rain

freezes before it lands ————— freezes after it lands

falls as ice ————— falls as very cold rain

happens during thunderstorms ——— happens during winter storms

pieces of ice ————— smooth layer of ice

causes danger and damage ——— causes danger and damage

ordered orbs

how hefty is your hail?

What You'll Need

- paper and pencil
- ruler
- As many of the following as you can gather:

baseball	pea
dime	penny
egg	quarter
golf ball	softball
grapefruit	tea cup
half dollar	tennis ball
marble	walnut
nickel	

22

1. Make a list of the objects you collected.

2. Guess how wide each object is. Write down each guess.

3. Put the objects in order. Place the smallest one first. Place the largest one last.

4. Measure each object. Write down its **width** next to your guess.

5. Compare the numbers. How did you do?

think about it

Which object would cause the most harm if it were a hailstone? Are some sizes more **dangerous**? Which ones?

glossary

crack – to break.

dangerous – able or likely to cause harm or injury.

droplet – a very small drop of liquid.

slippery – having a smooth, wet, icy, or oily surface that is easy to slide on.

width – the distance from one side of something to the other.